Australian Outback Safari

by Grace Hansen

Abdo
WORLD SAFARIS
Kids

Abdo Kids Jumbo is an Imprint of Abdo Kids
abdobooks.com

abdobooks.com

Published by Abdo Kids, a division of ABDO, P.O. Box 398166, Minneapolis, Minnesota 55439.

Printed in the United States of America, North Mankato, Minnesota.

052024

092024

THIS BOOK CONTAINS RECYCLED MATERIALS

Photo Credits: Getty Images, Shutterstock

Production Contributors: Teddy Borth, Jennie Forsberg, Grace Hansen
Design Contributors: Victoria Bates, Candice Keimig

Library of Congress Control Number: 2023948668

Publisher's Cataloging-in-Publication Data

Names: Hansen, Grace, author.

Title: Australian outback safari / by Grace Hansen

Description: Minneapolis, Minnesota : Abdo Kids, 2025 | Series: World safaris | Includes online resources and index.

Identifiers: ISBN 9798384900801 (lib. bdg.) | ISBN 9798384901501 (ebook) | ISBN 9798384901853 (Read-to-me eBook)

Subjects: LCSH: Safaris--Juvenile literature. | Natural areas--Juvenile literature. | Australia--Description and travel--Juvenile literature. | Wilderness areas--Juvenile literature. | Travel--Juvenile literature.

Classification: DDC 994--dc23

Table of Contents

Let's Go on Safari!

The Outback is a vast, **rural** area of Australia. Many animals call the Outback home. Let's go on an Outback safari!

Darwin
Australia
Alice Springs
Perth
Sydney
The Outback

A safari is a tour where people can see wild animals in their **habitats**. There are many ways to go on safari in Australia. Some people go by foot or by Jeep. Others go on safari by boat.

NAL PARK
ESERT
H.S. 64
97
23
Mt. Dare
HOTEL
Springs 170km

Australian Outback Animals

The woma python is **sacred** to the **Anangu** people of Central Australia. It is mainly awake at night. It can be tough to spot during the day.

The thorny devil spends its days catching ants with its sticky tongue. It has special body parts to help it take in water.

Red kangaroos are Australia's largest mammal. They live throughout most of the Outback.

Dingoes also live throughout the Outback. They can be seen traveling in **packs**.

Saltwater crocodiles live in the northern Australian Outback. They are the largest reptiles in the world! They are also very dangerous.

The frilled-neck lizard is also in the northern Outback. It can be spotted up in trees.

Emus are large, flightless birds of the Outback. Groups of emus can be seen **migrating** in summer and winter.

Outback Safari Experiences

Discover Termite Mounds
Litchfield
National Park

See the Devil's Marbles (Karlu Karlu)
Devil's Marbles
Conservation Reserve

Segway through Uluru
Uluru-Kata Tjuta
National Park

Take a Sunset Camel Ride
Cable Beach

Glossary

Anangu – the name used by several Aboriginal people, or native people, in Australia to describe themselves.

habitat – the natural environment of a plant or animal.

migrating – moving from one place to another, usually for food, water, weather, and other important reasons.

pack – a group of animals that are alike and stay together naturally.

rural – relating to a large area of land with few people and that is far away from cities.

sacred – highly valued and shown great respect, usually for religious reasons.

Index